Brighter Skies Ahead

Praise for Brighter Skies Ahead

"Deep in the frenzy of what Terri so eloquently calls the 'juggling act years', I had not taken much time to consider the seasons of life that come after this one. However, *Brighter Skies Ahead* isn't just for those who are already in their final seasons. It is full of advice, great ideas and inspiration for reflection for every stage of life. It's the blast of sunshine you would expect from Terri with an even more important 'winter life advisory' that I didn't even know I needed. It's been a blessing to have Terri as a mentor and now, thankfully, we all have access to her wisdom, wit and generosity."
—**Ginger Zee,** chief meteorologist at *ABC News*

"As parents, we often put our own dreams on the back-burner for a few decades so we can pour all of our energy into raising incredible kids. In *Brighter Skies Ahead*, DeBoer takes readers on an entertaining, uplifting, informative, and sometimes funny journey, encouraging them to 'Dream Big' as they empty the nest."
—**Bob Goff,** *New York Times* bestselling author of *Love Does, Everybody Always,* and *Dream Big*

"Providing a fresh, insightful, and honest look at the mixed emotions parents face when our young adults 'don't need us anymore,' DeBoer taps into the bittersweet moment we say goodbye, knowing life without them under our roof will never be quite the same, but also reminding us—and showing us—that our own futures are full of limitless possibilities. Engaging, relatable, and thoroughly entertaining."
—**Tracy Brogan,** *Wall Street Journal* and *USA Today* bestselling author and Amazon Publishing Diamond Award Winner for *Bell Harbor* and *Trillium Bay* series

"As a renowned meteorologist, Terri DeBoer knows how difficult it is to forecast each day of our weather. As a mother and Empty Nester, she also understands how hard it is to forecast life after your children grow up and leave home. *Brighter Skies Ahead* offers valuable lessons and deeply personal stories on how to navigate the seasons of our lives with hope, faith, wisdom, humor and inspiration. I predict it's going to be like a sunny day for countless readers."

—**Wade Rouse,** Internationally bestselling author of
The Clover Girls (Pen Name: Viola Shipman)

"As a working mother raising three children, we were running faster than I can now even imagine we were capable of, and then they left on their own life journeys. Terri's stories in *Brighter Skies Ahead* are so timely and inspirational! Just what my husband and I need as we settle down into our next phase of life, rediscovering each other and our evolving role as parents."

—**Cathy Cooper,** Meijer senior director of community partnerships and giving/executive director, Meijer LPGA Classic

"Anyone in the midst of empty-nesting will benefit from Terri DeBoer's *Brighter Skies Ahead*. This phase is a natural part of life, so the inspiration and wisdom in this accessible and easy-to-read collection of essays will get you going on *you* again, especially in a world where there's so much change for men and women everywhere."

—**David Morris,** former publisher, Zondervan Publishing

"Although my Empty Nest season started fourteen years ago, it didn't stop me from reading *Brighter Skies Ahead* now. I recognized myself throughout the book and wish it had been available when I was experiencing those Empty Nest feelings. I plan on gifting *Brighter Skies Ahead* at graduations—not for the graduates but the parents who will be entering the Empty Nest season with us.

—**Tricia L. McDonald,** owner/operator Splattered Ink Press, author of *Life With Sally* series, *Quit Whining Start Writing,* and *The Sally Squad: Pals to the Rescue*

"I have been blessed over my career to have the privilege of caring for women through all seasons of life, including the emotionally painful season of emptying the nest. I prescribe *Brighter Skies Ahead* as an encouraging, uplifting, informative, and entertaining collection of essays that will help parents as they enter a new, and sometimes reluctant stage of their lives."

—**Dr. Renee Elderkin**, OB/GYN, attending physician, University of Michigan Health-Metro Campus, associate professor at Michigan State University, active member on the Board of Obstetrics/Gynecology, active member, American College of Obstetrics/Gynecology

"In her debut book, *Brighter Skies Ahead*, Terri DeBoer takes the highs and lows of Empty Nesting and articulates these in a way to offer hope, joy, and love for what can sometimes be painful but also exciting times of life. DeBoer's book is her journey but gives us the read like *My Big Fat Greek Wedding* did in a movie . . . "I have been there, I can relate, I have felt that way, I can laugh at myself." I suggest find a cozy winter day, a sunny summer day, or a crisp fall/spring day to enjoy this must-read book!

—**Christy Buck,** executive director, Mental Health Foundation of West Michigan

"As a mother of five, the passage to a quieter house happens faster than you think. Time to adjust to new roles and rediscover yourself. Terri's stories provide support and strategies in establishing a fulfilling next phase of life."

—**Peaches McCahill,** president of The McCahill Group

"I've already experienced one of my three children flying the coop. The other two are close behind. And while I work in the field of discovering a fulfilling encore stage of life, and can speak on it objectively, I hadn't found a resource to really help me personally navigate this stage in life until now. In *Brighter Skies Ahead,* Terri provides a light and thought-provoking guide that will help Empty Nesters (and those of us who are soon-to-be Empty Nesters) make this transition a little less daunting."

—**Jennifer Feuerstein,** associate state director, AARP Michigan

"We will each experience the process of emptying our nest in a different way and in our own time. In *Brighter Skies Ahead,* Terri takes us through many aspects of that change, helping to identify things that are most relevant for you in building a happy and productive next phase of life."

—**Julie A. Brinks,** vice president and general manager,
WOOD-TV/WOTV/WXSP

"Terri has been forecasting her whole life, and in this new season as an Empty Nester and a grandpa, *Brighter Skies Ahead* is a must-read on my list for what lies ahead! We adapt to any weather; we can do the same for the Empty Nest season."

—**Rick Vuyst,** business owner, "Baby Bloomer,"
author, radio host at WOOD Radio

"I've worked with Terri professionally for decades and have always marveled at her positive attitude. Couple that attitude with her inquisitive nature as a scientist, and she made *Brighter Skies Ahead* a comprehensive and intuitive compilation of advice for what turned out to be a difficult period for my wife and me *spot on*. Thank you, Terri!"

—**Steve Kelly,** radio host for WOOD Radio Morning Show

Brighter Skies Ahead

Forecasting a Full Life
When You Empty the Nest

TERRI DeBOER

NASHVILLE

NEW YORK • LONDON • MELBOURNE • VANCOUVER

Brighter Skies Ahead
Companion Journal

© 2022 Terri DeBoer

Unless otherwise noted, Scriptures are taken from the Holy Bible, New International Version®, NIV®. Copyright © 1973, 1978, 1984, 2011 by Biblica, Inc.™ Used by permission of Zondervan. All rights reserved worldwide. www.zondervan.com. The "NIV" and "New International Version" are trademarks registered in the United States Patent and Trademark Office by Biblica, Inc.™

Scripture quotations marked MSG are taken from THE MESSAGE, copyright © 1993, 2002, 2018 by Eugene H. Peterson. Used by permission of NavPress, represented by Tyndale House Publishers. All rights reserved.

Published in New York, New York, by Morgan James Publishing. Morgan James is a trademark of Morgan James, LLC. www.MorganJamesPublishing.com

Morgan James BOGO™

A **FREE** ebook edition is available for you or a friend with the purchase of this print book.

CLEARLY SIGN YOUR NAME ABOVE

Instructions to claim your free ebook edition:
1. Visit MorganJamesBOGO.com
2. Sign your name CLEARLY in the space above
3. Complete the form and submit a photo of this entire page
4. You or your friend can download the ebook to your preferred device

ISBN 9781631956959 paperback
Library of Congress Control Number: 2021941763

Cover and Interior Design by:
Chris Treccani
www.3dogcreative.net

Morgan James is a proud partner of Habitat for Humanity Peninsula and Greater Williamsburg. Partners in building since 2006.

Get involved today! Visit
MorganJamesPublishing.com/giving-back

This journal belongs to

_____

_____

_____

For all the people in my life who give me
so much to write about and remember.

My incredible family.

My wonderful friends, past, present, and future.

Though my nest is emptier, my heart and life are
filled with gratitude and love.

Table of Contents

Introduction

Our lives are filled with a series of moments. Some of the high points are etched in our memories—never to be forgotten. In other instances, outstanding times may draw our attention only for a brief period. We may occasionally look at a picture, or perhaps hear a song, and for those moments, we are transported back in time to when we originally experienced a certain event or feeling.

In my life, I look at life as a series of memorable moments. There are high points in each day, with at least one thing that could be pointed to each day to remind us how we spent those precious hours or minutes or seconds.

In my book, *Brighter Skies Ahead: Forecasting A Full Life When You Empty The Nest,* I wrote fifty short essays that chronicle different stages and transitions into the season of life referred to as "The Empty Nest."

When I was writing those essays, I regretted that I had not taken the time to write daily in a journal as my children were growing up so that I could look back on daily notes about how I spent those thirty years with a very full nest.

I now have a commitment to daily journaling that is fairly recent. My daily journaling started at the beginning of 2019, when I purchased a five-year journal that has spots for five years' worth of memories, one for each day. Each page is dedicated to a day of the year, with sections on each page for years one, two, three, four, and five. Each year only has gets six lines, so the journal entries for each day only have space for jotting down brief notes that would trigger the memories of what I was doing on that day.

2021 is "year three" for my journal!

This journal has been both a great exercise and resource for me. The first year of entries took place well before the world had ever heard of COVID-19. Year two was 2020, and I was able to chronicle each day as the pandemic began and eventually led to the series of shut downs and cancellations in our state and country, as well as in countries around the world.

2020 was also the year I began to write the book on which this companion journal is based.

Maybe you already keep a journal. If so, you are familiar with the wonderful emotions that come from being able to read the stories of a particular day or an event in your life in your own words and in your own handwriting.

If that's you, I hope you find value in the use of this journal. But, if you are not someone who has kept a journal before, I highly encourage you to take the first step forward with this journal.

I will give you prompts for each entry and things to consider. A week from now, a year from now, or even a decade from now, you will be able to pick up this book and read at least part of your history.

Getting Started on a New Reality

A Blank Page.

An Empty Canvas.

A "Nothing-Do-Do" List.

A "Nobody-Needs-Me" Afternoon.

Ask most creative or busy people about the biggest fears in life, and the answers will likely be found in that list above. The thought of having "nothing" as a starting point is often the greatest challenge to face.

Pivoting to life as an Empty Nester creates a similar challenge.

When "having too much to do and not enough hours in the day" is replaced by "not having anything to do and too many hours in the day," it's tempting to feel as though our purpose in life is gone.

The reality is, the most difficult time for an Empty Nester is the time of transition.

A time of change.

We are letting go of one reality—a time of having all (or at least most of) our time committed to doing things for other people—

and we are moving toward this new reality, one where we now have plenty of time in our day and also the energy (and other resources) that we can invest in doing things for *OURSELVES*.

But, where do we start on that journey?

Most parents will devote at least two decades of their lives to raising a child from birth to young adulthood. For parents who have multiple children, that timeline can extend to three or even four decades. Parenthood has become a job, a vocation, a calling, a hobby, a way of life.

What happens when the nest empties?

This can be an exciting time in life—almost like a time of new beginnings.

I have spent my professional life as a television meteorologist in Western Michigan, where the only constant to the weather is change. I find similarities in tracking weather events and life events. The most violent and turbulent weather occurs during the times of transition.

So much of life's journey unfolds in the same way. The times of transition are the most difficult.

Like *Brighter Skies Ahead*, this journal is divided into nine separate sections, with the thoughts, exercises, and opportunities for reflection in this journal designed to provide you with a framework to navigate your transitional period and help you discover your own "what's next" in life.

PART 1

---•---

The Grass is Greener in the Rearview Mirror

*Life is divided into three terms—that which was,
which is and which will be
Let us learn from the past to profit by the present,
and from the present, to live better in the future.*
William Wordsworth

This section of the journal invites you to take a "trip down memory lane."

Get ready for a reality check of sorts, as the difficulty in transitioning into the Empty Nest stage (or in transitioning from any season to the next) often makes the memories of the past seem like the "glory days."

In these pages, let's unwrap those memories and try to reconnect with the reality of the chaos and exhaustion of those days and years spent living in the whirlwind of a "full nest."

Get ready to connect with yourself before "Mom" was your name.

Who were you before you were a mom? Open an old photo album and find yourself in pictures from when you were in elementary school or high school. Try to remember what *you* wanted to do or be "when you grew up."

_____

_____

_____

_____

_____

_____

_____

_____

_____

_____

_____

_____

_____

_____

_____

_____

_____

_____

_____

_____

_____

Many people will never learn the lessons meant for them in this lifetime, nor become the person they were meant to be, simply because they are too busy being someone else.

—Suzy Kassem

Describe your philosophy regarding change. Are you a creature of habit? Do you like things to happen the same way all the time? How do you react when change happens *to* you, especially in an area where you were happy with the "status quo?"

_____

_____

_____

_____

_____

_____

_____

_____

_____

_____

_____

_____

_____

_____

_____

_____

_____

_____

All changes, even the most longed for, have their melancholy,
for what we leave behind us is a part of ourselves; we must die to
one life before we can enter into another.
—Anatole France

Take a look back at pictures from big moments in the life of your family as your child (or children) were growing up. Now, think back to the challenges and sacrifices going on at the same time.

_____

_____

_____

_____

_____

_____

_____

_____

_____

_____

_____

_____

_____

_____

_____

_____

_____

_____

_____

_____

_____

_____

Take care of all your memories. For you cannot relive them.

—Bob Dylan

With every ending there is a new beginning. Think back to the time when each child moved away from home for the first time. Write a column of "lasts" and "firsts" related to that transition (e.g., the last time giving hugs before bedtime, the first opportunity to schedule Sunday dinners, the last time of scheduling all of your vacation around a school calendar, the first time of scheduling vacations when you really want to travel.)

_____

_____

_____

_____

_____

_____

_____

_____

_____

_____

_____

_____

_____

_____

_____

_____

_____

_____

The secret of CHANGE is to focus all of your energy not on fighting the old, but on building the new.

—Socrates

Think back to the time you discovered you were expecting your child. Write down the things you had to do to prepare for parenthood. Now, make a list to prepare for the Empty Nest season.

_____

_____

_____

_____

_____

_____

_____

_____

_____

_____

_____

_____

_____

_____

_____

_____

_____

_____

_____

_____

_____

Without leaps of imagination or dreaming, we lose the excitement of possibilities. Dreaming, after all, is a form of planning.

—Gloria Steinem

"Essential Workers" was a category for certain jobs deemed necessary during the COVID-19 pandemic. In the "full nest," parents fall into that category. Do you still feel essential? Why or why not?

_____

_____

_____

_____

_____

_____

_____

_____

_____

_____

_____

_____

_____

_____

_____

_____

_____

_____

_____

_____

Parenting is a lifetime job and does not stop
when a child grows up.

—Jake Slope

PART 2

—•—

Birds of a Feather

*A friend is one that knows you as you are, understands
where you have been, accepts what you have become,
and still, allows you to grow.*

William Shakespeare

In this section, we are going to examine friendships.

For so much of our life with a "full nest," the people we spent the most time with were often the parents of the other children in our children's activities.

- Dance Moms
- Sports Moms
- Band Moms
- Drama Moms
- Choir Moms

In these relationships, *we* didn't have the luxury of choosing these individuals; it was more like an "arranged marriage." Since we all had kids with common interests, these relationships had, at their nucleus, parents who were committed to providing developmental and recreational experiences for their children.

Many of these relationships were "fleeting," as the timeline of the activity was typically finite, which means many of us changed the people we spent the most time with more often that we purchased new underwear!

In the Empty Nest, this is changing. We now have greater control of and more input in choosing the *who* and *why* of these special relationships.

Choose wisely.

Think about the people you spent the most time with when your kids were growing up. Were most of your hours spent with people who were in your life due to convenience or your kids' activities? Are there people from the elementary, middle, or high school years whom you miss?

_____

_____

_____

_____

_____

_____

_____

_____

_____

_____

_____

_____

_____

_____

_____

_____

_____

_____

_____

_____

Many people will walk in and out of your life, but only true friends will leave footprints in your heart.

—Eleanor Roosevelt

Think about your current friendships. Do you spend time with people who don't inspire you to be your best? Imagine how your life may improve if you eliminate toxic relationships and spend that time with people who inspire you to be a better human being. Journal about a time when someone inspired you to be your best. How did it make you feel? What traits were present in that person?

_____

_____

_____

_____

_____

_____

_____

_____

_____

_____

_____

_____

_____

_____

_____

_____

_____

_____

Pay no attention to toxic words. What people say
is often a reflection of themselves, not you.
—Christian Baloga

Do you have a friend who is struggling with a big decision? How can you provide perspective and wisdom to help your friend find peace in making this decision?

_____

_____

_____

_____

_____

_____

_____

_____

_____

_____

_____

_____

_____

_____

_____

_____

Good advice is priceless. Not what you want to hear,
but what you need to hear. Not imaginary, but practical.
Not based on fear, but on possibility. Not designed to make you
feel better, designed to make you better. Seek it out and embrace
the true friends that care enough to risk sharing it. I'm not sure
what takes more guts—giving it or getting it.

—Seth Godin

Do you have a painful or difficult time of the day when the Empty Nest seems to cave in around you? What activities can you plan during that time to ease the loneliness?

_____

_____

_____

_____

_____

_____

_____

_____

_____

_____

_____

_____

_____

_____

_____

_____

_____

_____

_____

_____

_____

_____

There is no pleasure in having nothing to do;
the fun is having lots to do and not doing it.

—Andrew Jackson

Do you have a dream to accomplish something special? Write out your dream. Who can you reach out to for help, inspiration, advice, or motivation?

_____

_____

_____

_____

_____

_____

_____

_____

_____

_____

_____

_____

_____

_____

_____

_____

_____

_____

_____

_____

_____

_____

I knew when I met you an adventure was going to happen.

—Winnie the Pooh

When you think of the special relationships in your life, who are your enduring friends? Describe the life journey you have traveled with these people. If you have not spoken to them or seen them recently, how can you make a priority to reconnect soon.

_____

_____

_____

_____

_____

_____

_____

_____

_____

_____

_____

_____

_____

_____

_____

_____

_____

_____

_____

_____

Long friendships are like jewels, polished over time
to become beautiful and enduring.
—Celia Brayfield

Do you have a pet? If your Empty Nest is lacking energy and you need to feel needed, how do you think a pet, specifically a dog, may bring new life and a new relationship to your home?

_____

_____

_____

_____

_____

_____

_____

_____

_____

_____

_____

_____

_____

_____

_____

_____

_____

_____

_____

_____

_____

*A dog is the only thing on earth that loves you
more than he loves himself.*

—Josh Billings

Do you have relationships with people who are at least a couple of decades older than you? What benefits do you think a multi-generational friendship could bring to your life? What could you bring into the life of an older person?

_____

_____

_____

_____

_____

_____

_____

_____

_____

_____

_____

_____

_____

_____

_____

_____

_____

_____

You make friends with older people, and you will
always feel young, no matter what.
—Mel Brooks

Do you have friends you have met through social media support/private groups? What do you feel comfortable sharing with people you know you will never meet? Describe the comfort in knowing strangers who live in other places are facing similar struggles and challenges as you. If you don't engage in this practice, consider joining a social media support group, at least to observe for a bit.

_____

_____

_____

_____

_____

_____

_____

_____

_____

_____

_____

_____

_____

_____

_____

_____

*The measure of a friendship is not its physicality
but its significance. Good friendships, online or off, urge us
toward empathy; they give us comfort and also pull us
out of the prisons of ourselves.*
—John Green

PART 3

•

The Actual Nest

*A house is made of walls and beams; a home is made
of hopes and dreams.*
Unknown Author

In this section, we are digging into our surroundings; our actual living spaces.

When our nest is full, the status of our living space can create anxiety and stress. Let's face it: The nest is not only filled with energy and noise, but the by-products are:

- Mess
- Clutter
- Spills
- Disorganization
- Garbage
- Dirt
- Unpleasant Smells

As the matriarch of the full nest, we can feel like a maid and house-keeper. We are nearly always fighting a losing battle trying to keep a neat (or at least presentable) home.

Now, the nest is empty. The order we once craved can make the walls seem to close in on us.

Not only is your empty nest much cleaner and more organized, many of us treat it like it is a time capsule of sorts. Inside this nest resides a collection of keepsakes, trophies, and photos that are frozen in time—locked in place to preserve the memories and capture the feelings of a moment or era.

Consider the *freedom* you now experience in the Empty Nest stage.

What changes in your habitat do you now have the flexibility and luxury of making?

Walk around your house and consider the style of your decor. Is your home decorated the way *you* would like, or have you settled into a comfortable set of surroundings, which had simply been functional. What changes would you like to make? (If you are stuck trying to find ideas, just open Pinterest and type in names of rooms; allow yourself to dream!)

_____

_____

_____

_____

_____

_____

_____

_____

_____

_____

_____

_____

_____

_____

_____

_____

_____

_____

_____

_____

As we evolve, our homes should too.

—Suzanne Tucker

Think about your dream living space. Do you feel like you are ready to move to a "new nest?" Are you ready to down-size or right-size? Are you ready to ditch suburbia for a downtown condo? Would you like to move from a neighborhood to the country? Are the memories of your "full nest" keeping you from finding a more suitable living space?

_____

_____

_____

_____

_____

_____

_____

_____

_____

_____

_____

_____

_____

_____

_____

You have brains in your head. You have feet in your shoes.
You can steer yourself any direction you choose.
You're on your own. And you know what you know.
And YOU are the one who'll decide where to go . . .
—Dr. Seuss, *Oh, The Places You'll Go.*

Time for truth. What climate do you want to live in? Is it too cloudy where you live? Is it too cold? Too warm? Do you hate winter? Are you ready to become a snow-bird? Describe your dream locale in detail. Write down the steps you would have to take to spend time in a dream location on a regular basis. What is a realistic timeline for making it a reality?

_____

_____

_____

_____

_____

_____

_____

_____

_____

_____

_____

_____

_____

_____

_____

_____

_____

_____

If we were meant to stay in one place,
we'd have roots instead of feet . . .
—Rachel Wolchin

PART 4

—•—

Self-Improvement Time

Only put off until tomorrow what you are
willing to die having left undone.
Pablo Picasso

In this section, it is time to start focusing on *ourselves*.

When our nest is full, it's easy to neglect our dreams and desires because the limited resources of time, money, and *energy* are being poured into the lives of others. We gladly put ourselves on the "back burner" so we can devote everything to our families. Now that they are "moving on" and becoming the independent adults we have raised them to be . . . it's time to *look in the mirror*!

What do *we* want to do with our lives?

- Education
- Vocation
- Hobbies
- Dreams
- Desires

It's time to MOVE FORWARD!

What do you want for your life as you now have the flexibility and luxury of creating something new?

When you were becoming a young adult, what was your process for trying to find a path that would be interesting and fulfilling? How can you incorporate that strategy into finding purpose in the Empty Nest?

_____

_____

_____

_____

_____

_____

_____

_____

_____

_____

_____

_____

_____

_____

_____

_____

_____

_____

_____

_____

The greatest discovery in life is self-discovery. Until you find yourself you will always be someone else. Become yourself.
—Myles Munroe

How big (or small) is your sense of adventure? Think back to the time when you graduated from high school, and try to connect with the "you" of that year. What comes to mind now when you imagine an adventure?

_____

_____

_____

_____

_____

_____

_____

_____

_____

_____

_____

_____

_____

_____

_____

_____

_____

_____

_____

_____

_____

If happiness is the goal—and it should be—then adventures
should be a priority.
—Richard Branson

Is there something you have always wanted to study? Did you finish your college degree? Would you like to get an advanced degree? Think about what you could study that would excite or motivate you and write out some goals!

_____

_____

_____

_____

_____

_____

_____

_____

_____

_____

_____

_____

_____

_____

_____

_____

_____

_____

_____

_____

_____

It is never too late to be what you might have been.

—George Elliot

Would you like to make a career change? If you have been a "stay-at-home" parent, is this the time to take your incredible skillset into the workforce? Would you like to start a business? Describe what it would entail, and how you would feel once you make this change.

_____

_____

_____

_____

_____

_____

_____

_____

_____

_____

_____

_____

_____

_____

_____

_____

_____

_____

_____

_____

You are never too old to set another goal or
to dream a new dream.
—C.S. Lewis

Now that you have time to devote to your own interests, is there a hobby you have always wanted to pursue? What would you want to learn (or learn to do better), if you could devote the time and money and energy that you used to spend on your children?

_____

_____

_____

_____

_____

_____

_____

_____

_____

_____

_____

_____

_____

_____

_____

_____

_____

_____

_____

_____

_____

To be really happy and really safe, one ought to have at least two
or three hobbies, and they must all be real.

—Winston Churchill

How easy is it for you to spend time alone? How would you describe the difference between being alone and being lonely? Write about a time you experienced both and offer yourself some strategies to stay engaged while still enjoying alone time.

_____

_____

_____

_____

_____

_____

_____

_____

_____

_____

_____

_____

_____

_____

_____

_____

_____

_____

_____

_____

I think it is very healthy to spend time alone. You need to know how to be alone and not defined by another person.

—Oscar Wilde

Is there something you have always wanted to accomplish? What dream is in your heart but was put on the back burner after thinking it was not going to happen for you? Write down five tangible steps you could take to get started.

_____

_____

_____

_____

_____

_____

_____

_____

_____

_____

_____

_____

_____

_____

_____

_____

_____

_____

_____

_____

_____

_____

_____

You don't have to see the whole staircase; just take the first step.
—Martin Luther King, Jr.

PART 5

—•—

Forecasting a Healthier You

Our bodies are our gardens. Our wills are our gardeners.
William Shakespeare

In this section, it is time to start focusing on *our physical health.*

For many of us, the Juggling Act season involved providing plenty of opportunities for our kids to be physically fit. Our aerobic activities may have consisted of shivering in the bleachers of our youngsters' sporting events during inclement weather or doing battle with the steering wheel while driving yet another leg of the carpool.

Just a few of the personal, physical sacrifices may have included:

- Sleep
- Physical Exercise
- Nutritious Meals

Since most of us were in our twenties, thirties, and maybe forties when we had full nests, we would often short-change our own health without always noticing the impact. The Empty Nest season has us shifting through the late forties, fifties, and sixties, with the signs of aging becoming easier to see *and feel.*

During the Empty Nest season, caring for our bodies can and should become a greater priority. This transition gives us the time, resources, and energy to take better care of ourselves.

Are you ready to make your own health a priority?

How do you *feel* physically? Do you have aches and pains on a regular basis? Do you get tired quickly while engaging in minor activities? Is there an activity or exercise routine you could commit to doing on a regular basis?

_____

_____

_____

_____

_____

_____

_____

_____

_____

_____

_____

_____

_____

_____

_____

_____

_____

_____

Nothing matters more than your health. Healthy living is priceless. What millionaire wouldn't pay dearly for an extra ten or twenty years of healthy aging?

—Peter Diamandis

How much consideration do you give to your eating? Is your food plan better or worse in the Empty Nest compared to the time when you had more mouths to feed? What would it take for you to commit to healthier eating?

_____

_____

_____

_____

_____

_____

_____

_____

_____

_____

_____

_____

_____

_____

_____

_____

_____

_____

The food you eat can either be the safest and most powerful form of medicine or the slowest form of poison.

—Ann Wigmore

Think about your dedication to physical activity. Is there something you loved to do *before children*? Is there something you could commit to doing at least thirty minutes a day, five days a week? Think about and journal about what's stopping you from becoming the best version of yourself (dig deeply here)!

_____

_____

_____

_____

_____

_____

_____

_____

_____

_____

_____

_____

_____

_____

_____

_____

_____

_____

Lack of activity destroys the good condition of every
human being, while movement and methodical physical exercise
save it and preserve it.

—Plato

Do you get enough sleep? Now that the barriers to getting a good night sleep are gone in the Empty Nest, how do you make sure you schedule your routine so that getting essential sleep is a priority? How can you make resting your body a priority?

_____

_____

_____

_____

_____

_____

_____

_____

_____

_____

_____

_____

_____

_____

_____

_____

_____

_____

_____

_____

_____

_____

_____

Not getting enough sleep can also cause depression and bad moods,
which can lead to overeating.

—Jorge Cruise

PART 6

•

Natural Resources

"As you grow older, you will discover that you have two hands: one for helping yourself, the other for helping others."
Audrey Hepburn

In this section, it is time to start focusing on our ABUNDANCE!

For many of us, the Empty Nest season might just be the first time in our adult lives when we discover we have "left-over" resources!

Similar to the food that is packaged up after a nice meal to be enjoyed later, we actually have extra helpings of those things that were in such scarce supply during the Young Adult and Juggling Act seasons!

Those left-overs may include extra:

- $$$ (Money)
- Free Time
- Hours for Volunteering
- Opportunities to become Mentors

It's almost one of life's greatest ironies for parents: when our nests were full, we were short of time, money and energy. For many of us, the Juggling Act season was the time when we were stretching all of our budgets to meet all of our obligations: ranging from finances to hours in the day. As we advanced in our careers, we often began to make more money and work fewer hours to meet our obligations.

In the Empty Nest season, are those scarce resources now more abundant?

How can we be generous to our adult children?

How can we make life easier for others we know who could be blessed by us?

What does your financial budget look like in the Empty Nest? Do you remember how challenging it was to stretch the dollar during the Juggling Act season? Think about a young person or young family who might be struggling; or a maybe someone older? How can you be a blessing?

_____

_____

_____

_____

_____

_____

_____

_____

_____

_____

_____

_____

_____

_____

_____

_____

_____

_____

Don't tell me where your priorities are. Show me where you spend your money and I'll tell you where they are.

—James W. Frick

Do you think about how you are spending your free time? Those "after-school" hours or "evening" hours that were spent on your kids during the Juggling Act season might now be free. Are you investing those hours into productivity or recreation or ***squandering*** them?

_____

_____

_____

_____

_____

_____

_____

_____

_____

_____

_____

_____

_____

_____

_____

_____

_____

_____

No such thing as spare time, no such thing as free time,
no such thing as down time.
All you got is life time. GO!
—Henry Rollins

Do you have a "passion" for a certain organization, project or cause? How can you devote your new freedom to helping improve life for others? Write down a list of five specific causes you would like to help. Make a plan to reach out; get connected and begin to serve!

_____

_____

_____

_____

_____

_____

_____

_____

_____

_____

_____

_____

_____

_____

_____

_____

_____

_____

_____

_____

The best way to find yourself is to lose yourself
in the service of others.
—Mahatma Gandhi

As Empty Nesters, it's easy to feel like we don't want to give uninvited advice to our adult children, but just one look around at our surroundings will give us a glimpse of people living in the Young Adult season who would love our input! Who are those people in your world who would *love* your advice, wisdom, and inspiration? How can you serve them today?

_____

_____

_____

_____

_____

_____

_____

_____

_____

_____

_____

_____

_____

_____

_____

_____

_____

A mentor is someone who allows you to see
the hope inside yourself.
—Oprah Winfrey

PART 7

———•———

It Can't Be Sunny All Of The Time

Mental pain is less dramatic than physical pain, but it is more common and also more hard to bear. The frequent attempt to conceal mental pain increases the burden: it is easier to say, "My tooth is aching," than to say, "My heart is broken."

C.S. Lewis

In this section, it is time to start focusing on our mental health!

For many of us, the quietness of the Empty Nest season might just reveal an uneasiness in our lives. Any mental health challenges during the Juggling Act season may have been masked by the chaos of the never-ending list of activities and things on our to-do lists.

What do we do when the emotional struggle is real, and there are no distractions?

Those challenges include some of these physical, emotional, and mental health issues:

- Grief
- Guilt
- Regret
- Menopause

In this section, you will reflect on these painful emotions and find a way to find hope, grace, and peace in the next season in life!

How do you treat *yourself?* A dynamic mental health organization in Western Michigan invites everyone to take the "be nice." pledge. Notice. Invite. Challenge. Empower.

How we treat people impacts how they THINK, ACT, and FEEL.

This includes *ourselves*! Consider how you treat yourself and jot down a few things you've done to neglect yourself and a few things you can do to take care of or treat yourself.

_____

_____

_____

_____

_____

_____

_____

_____

_____

_____

_____

_____

_____

What mental health needs is more sunlight, more candor,
and more unashamed conversation.
—Glenn Close

Can you feel the natural cycles of aging? How did (is) menopause impact(ing) your life? Do you feel out of sorts and unbalanced at times, not able to point to an explanation? Use this space to write out what you're feeling and experiencing; try to name the emotions and describe the physical changes.

_____

_____

_____

_____

_____

_____

_____

_____

_____

_____

_____

_____

_____

_____

_____

_____

_____

_____

_____

_____

_____

_____

There is no more creative force in the world than
the menopausal woman with zest.
—Margaret Mead

Have you thought about your sadness and emptiness in the Empty Nest in terms of grief? When you lose someone or something you love, there are five stages in the grieving process: denial, anger, bargaining, depression, and acceptance. Take the time to consider where you are in this natural cycle. If you are new to the Empty Nest, take comfort in knowing those feelings of melancholy are normal. It's a process . . . but you will feel joy again.

_____

_____

_____

_____

_____

_____

_____

_____

_____

_____

_____

_____

_____

_____

_____

_____

_____

_____

No one ever told me that grief felt so much like fear.
—C.S. Lewis

Think back to the time when you were "leaving the nest." Can you remember how you thought about or treated your mom? Did she suffer or seem sad? How did you watch her make the transition you are making now. If she is still alive, ask her to tell you *her* Empty Nest story. Write down anything that interests, impresses, or inspires you.

_____

_____

_____

_____

_____

_____

_____

_____

_____

_____

_____

_____

_____

_____

_____

_____

_____

_____

Leaving home in a sense involves a second kind of birth
in which we give birth to ourselves.
—Robert Neelly Bellah

When you look back at the chaotic and busy time during the years when your nest was full, do you dwell on memories of times when you felt as though you failed? Instead of keeping those painful thoughts in your head, write them down. Be specific. What would you need to do to give yourself grace about those times?

_____

_____

_____

_____

_____

_____

_____

_____

_____

_____

_____

_____

_____

_____

_____

_____

_____

_____

Guilt says, "You failed." Shame says, "You're a failure."
Grace says, "Your failures are forgiven."
—Lecrae

PART 8

•

Flying Lessons

Autumn leaves don't fall, they fly. They take their time and wander on this their only chance to soar.

Delia Owens, *Where the Crawdads Sing*

In this section, the focus turns to the relationships that change and those that are newly formed as our children are flying away from our nest and creating nests of their own!

This part of the journey may surprise you with how many emotional ups and downs come during your family's evolution. As our children leave home to become the independent adults we always hoped, the nature of our relationship with them and the people in their lives *must* transform.

For even the closest families, this time of transition will come with struggles and challenges as adult children forge new relationships with people who will replace us in their daily lives and regular routines.

These new relationships may include:

- Significant Others
- Spouses
- Friendships
- Children

In this section, you will reflect on these developing relationships and discover a way to embrace this "new normal" and celebrate the milestones that will physically and emotionally mark this time of transition.

How would you describe your relationship with your adult child(ren)? If you aren't satisfied with the relationship, what could you do to change the dynamic? Be specific. Ask your adult child(ren) to describe the relationship they want to have with you. How can you make that happen?

_____

_____

_____

_____

_____

_____

_____

_____

_____

_____

_____

_____

_____

_____

_____

Something I have learned . . . how not to treat my grown kids and their spouses. Yes, granted, my children will always be babies in my eyes, but when they are grown adults with beliefs and values all their own, I have to be able to respect that. Though they may not follow what I feel to be right, having a lasting, loving relationship with my children, their spouses, and my grandchildren will be valued more in my heart than what I might believe to be right.

—Monica Lawrence

Think about the actual, physical move out of the nest. How did you react? What were your emotions? Were you afraid that your birds weren't ready to fly? Did you feel confident they were ready to "go it alone?" How did you celebrate their independence?

_____

_____

_____

_____

_____

_____

_____

_____

_____

_____

_____

_____

_____

_____

_____

_____

_____

_____

There are two times when parenting is the most difficult:
when the baby first arrives at home and when the
adult first leaves the home.

—Jennifer Quinn

Is your nest still too full? Is your adult child still living at home? What is the relationship dynamic if your twenty-something, thirty-something, or even forty-something is still living under your roof?

_____

_____

_____

_____

_____

_____

_____

_____

_____

_____

_____

_____

_____

_____

_____

_____

_____

However painful the process of leaving home, for parents and children, the really frightening thing for both would be the prospect of the child never leaving home.

—Robert Neelly Bellah

Do you have a married son or daughter? How did you view your role as "mother of the bride/groom?" If your adult child(ren) are not married yet, write a list of expectations and visions you have for yourself during the planning process and on that special day.

Remember, it's not about *you*!

_____

_____

_____

_____

_____

_____

_____

_____

_____

_____

_____

_____

_____

_____

_____

_____

_____

_____

When somebody else's happiness is your happiness, that is love.
—Lana Del Rey

Are you lucky enough to be a member of the "Grandparent Club?" What is your role as a grandparent? Do you enforce the parenting rules of your adult child? How do you handle it when you have a difference of opinion about parenting styles and philosophies?

_____

_____

_____

_____

_____

_____

_____

_____

_____

_____

_____

_____

_____

_____

_____

_____

_____

_____

_____

_____

_____

*Grandchildren are the dots that connect the lines
from generation to generation.*

—Lois Wyse

PART 9

•

Bless This Nest

. . . as for me and my house, we will serve the Lord.
Joshua 24:15

In this section, the focus turns to our spiritual lives. I have found my faith journey to be the most personal of any relationship in my life; perhaps you have found that in your spiritual walk as well. I'm discovering that the solitude of the Empty Nest season provides the perfect opportunity to dedicate myself to my relationship with my Heavenly Father.

For some families, the Growing Up and Juggling Act seasons may have focused the family's spiritual life on activities for the children to engage in a faith journey—Sunday School, Catechism, youth groups, etc. Perhaps there were public events to mark the beginning of what you hoped would be a life-long faith journey for your child, such as a baptism or First Communion.

For some families, the "busy-ness" of the Juggling Act season created obstacles for regular participation in church or religious activities. Youth sports, dance competitions, and other commitments may have taken over every day of the week, including Sundays, for those chaotic years.

Whatever your spiritual journey may have been during the time when your nest was full, the often quiet and less eventful reality of this season provides plenty of time for deepening your faith or perhaps discovering faith for the first time.

These opportunities may include:

- Visiting other churches or denominations
- Joining a Bible study
- Volunteering at a local MOPS (Mothers of Preschoolers) chapter
- Attending a spiritual retreat or conference
- Going on a mission trip
- Dedicating regular time for prayer

In this section, you will reflect on opportunities for discovering or deepening a journey of faith. Life in a full nest often revolved around serving and blessing others. Opening your heart and soul to embrace the solitude and peaceful quiet in this stage of life can provide you with hope as you look for deeper meaning in life and in the time that is still to come.

How would you describe your spiritual life? Think back to your Growing Up years. What activities did you engage in to discover or deepen your faith? How can you connect to a deeper spiritual life in the Empty Nest season? If you have never had a walk of faith, is there someone you can reach out to for a conversation?

_____

_____

_____

_____

_____

_____

_____

_____

_____

_____

_____

_____

_____

_____

_____

_____

_____

_____

For God so loved the world that he gave his one and only Son,
that whoever believes in him shall not perish but have eternal life.
—John 3:16

During the Juggling Act years, personal time for Bible study may have seemed like a luxury. Now that your schedule is more flexible in the Empty Nest, what can you do to be more intentional about spending time studying God's Holy Word?

_____

_____

_____

_____

_____

_____

_____

_____

_____

_____

_____

_____

_____

_____

_____

_____

Blessed is the man who does not walk in the counsel of the wicked or stand in the way of sinners or sit in the seat of mockers. But his delight is in the law of the Lord, and on his law he meditates day and night. He is like a tree planted by streams of water, which yields its fruit in season and whose leaf does not wither.
Whatever he does prospers.

—Psalm 1:1–3

Are you familiar with the story of the Proverbs 31 woman? The Scriptures describe her as the wife, mother, and housekeeper who literally *does it all* . . . from cleaning the house to taking care of all of her family's needs! How have you transitioned from having too much to do and being constantly needed to having your hours filled with more free time and fewer duties? Do you know a young mom who is currently living in the Proverbs 31 whirlwind? How can you serve her?

_____

_____

_____

_____

_____

_____

_____

_____

_____

_____

_____

_____

_____

_____

_____

_____

Honor her for all that her hands have done, and let her works
bring her praise at the city gate.
—Proverbs 31:31

Does life in an Empty Nest find you searching for a purpose? Make a list of your interests, passions, and skills. How can you find an intersection of those three lists to plan activities that will excite you?

_____

_____

_____

_____

_____

_____

_____

_____

_____

_____

_____

_____

_____

_____

_____

_____

_____

_____

_____

_____

_____

For we are God's handiwork, created in Christ Jesus to do good works, which God prepared in advance for us to do.

—Ephesians 2:10

Make a list of your most common emotions. Are your thoughts filled with worry? Anxiety? Self-doubt? Depression? Lack of Purpose? The Bible warns these emotions can grow from seeds planted by the Devil. What are steps you can take to chase them away?

_____

_____

_____

_____

_____

_____

_____

_____

_____

_____

_____

_____

_____

_____

_____

_____

Peace I leave with you; my peace I give you.
I do not give to you as the world gives. Do not let your hearts
be troubled and do not be afraid.
—John 14:27

Do you have a "tribe" of fellow Christians in your life? Make a list of people who share your faith. Consider spending time together in a group for conversation, encouragement, and support.

_____

_____

_____

_____

_____

_____

_____

_____

_____

_____

_____

_____

_____

_____

_____

_____

_____

_____

_____

_____

_____

They devoted themselves to the apostles' teaching and to fellowship,
to the breaking of bread and to prayer.

—Acts 2:42

Consider what it means for you to pray? Does prayer seem like a solemn and intentional act of bowing your head and crossing your fingers? Or, does prayer seem like a perpetual conversation going on in your head? What do you share with God? Does prayer focus on your wants and needs, or is it a time for thanksgiving? He wants to hear it all! He loves us! Write an authentic, conversational prayer below. There is no wrong way to do it. Just be you.

_____

_____

_____

_____

_____

_____

_____

_____

_____

_____

_____

_____

_____

_____

Do not be anxious about anything, but in every situation, by prayer and petition, with thanksgiving, present your requests to God. And the peace of God, which transcends all understanding, will guard your hearts and your minds in Christ Jesus.

—Philippians 4:6–7

LETTERS TO ME

—●—

In the introduction to the book *Brighter Skies Ahead*, I borrowed a concept from Brad Paisley's popular country music song "Letter to Me," in which he takes listeners on a musical journey back in time to when he turned seventeen years old.

In the song, Paisley recalls formative experiences that seemed like incredible obstacles, like the time he ran out of gas while on a date with a girl he liked or when he got a ticket for running a stop sign. This song also talked about a special aunt who died much too soon. The lyrics are filled with other regrets, like wishing he would have taken Spanish or a typing class. The song also foretells his future family, of the woman who would become his wife and the mother of his children, whom he hadn't even *met* until several years after he graduated from high school.

The song became an anthem, with people all over the world using it as an inspiration to write their own "letters" to their younger selves. It was certainly a musical journey, revealing the brevity of life and the hope and promise that comes as the future unfolds.

In this section, I invite you to write letters to yourself through the decades. Depending on your age and stage of life, some of these letters will be looking back at the past, and others will be forward-looking.

As you write, explore your feelings and memories from each of these stages in life. Consider both the happy and challenging times.

How did you grow through each experience?

What would the *you* of today share with the *you* of that period in your life?

In this space, write a letter to yourself in your teens. In *Brighter Skies Ahead*, we refer to this stage as the Growing Up years. For most of us, these were emotional years. Perhaps you have blocked out some of the difficulties during this stage, but reconnecting with the "solo-player" that identified most of us in our teens will be valuable in the Empty Nest stage. The later part of the teen years marked a time of "new beginnings" as we graduated from high school and began the journey toward a life of independence. What are the similarities to your life today?

_____

_____

_____

_____

_____

_____

_____

_____

_____

_____

_____

_____

_____

_____

_____

_____

_____

_____

In this space, write a letter to yourself in your twenties. In *Brighter Skies Ahead*, we refer to this stage as a transitional time that takes us from the Growing Up years and into the Young Adult stage. Perhaps, for you, this was a time for college, launching a career, or getting married. For many of us, these were the years of "filling the nest," so the Juggling Act season may have just been getting underway. What were the sources of joy and pain during these years?

_____

_____

_____

_____

_____

_____

_____

_____

_____

_____

_____

_____

_____

_____

_____

_____

_____

_____

_____

_____

In this space, write a letter to yourself in your thirties. In *Brighter Skies Ahead*, we refer to this stage as the Juggling Act season. Was this a decade of having too much to do and not enough hours in the day? Was the budget often stretched to its limit? Were these the years when you took an extra few minutes in the shower, just to have a tiny bit of "alone time?"

What were the sources of joy and pain during these years?

_____

_____

_____

_____

_____

_____

_____

_____

_____

_____

_____

_____

_____

_____

_____

_____

_____

_____

_____

_____

In this space, write a letter to yourself in your forties. In *Brighter Skies Ahead*, we refer to this decade as a continuation of the Juggling Act season. Perhaps this is a decade where you become part of the "sandwich generation," caring for your aging parents as you also care for a growing family. If you started filling your nest in your twenties, this is also the decade where your nest begins to empty. What were the sources of joy and pain during these years?

_____

_____

_____

_____

_____

_____

_____

_____

_____

_____

_____

_____

_____

_____

_____

_____

_____

_____

_____

_____

_____

_____

_____

In this space, write a letter to yourself in your fifties. In *Brighter Skies Ahead*, we refer to this stage as a transitional time that takes us from the Juggling Act season into the Empty Nest season. For some of you, this section will involve writing about what's happening right now. For others, it will mean looking to the past. Some of you will use this section to write about the future. What are/were the sources of joy and pain during these years?

_____

_____

_____

_____

_____

_____

_____

_____

_____

_____

_____

_____

_____

_____

_____

_____

_____

_____

_____

_____

In this space, write a letter to yourself in your sixties. In *Brighter Skies Ahead*, we refer to this stage as the time when almost all of us are Empty Nesters. This is also likely a time when you may begin to lose important people in your life, a time when your own mortality becomes very real. What are/were the sources of joy and pain during these years? (If you are writing this section to your future self, what achievements do you hope you will have accomplished)

_____

_____

_____

_____

_____

_____

_____

_____

_____

_____

_____

_____

_____

_____

_____

_____

_____

_____

In this space, write a letter to yourself in your seventies. If you are currently in this stage, *thank you* for participating in this journal. If you are looking ahead to this decade of life, how do you hope the later years in your life will unfold? Perhaps you will have a vibrant nest again, filled with grandchildren who are in the Growing Up stage, your home once again a special sanctuary.

_____

_____

_____

_____

_____

_____

_____

_____

_____

_____

_____

_____

_____

_____

_____

_____

_____

_____

_____

_____

In this space, write a letter to yourself in your eighties. In the conclusion of *Brighter Skies Ahead*, I wrote a "letter" to myself in my mid-eighties. In my letter, I outlined all of those goals and ambitious plans I had made for myself. Think of a big goal you want to accomplish, and write a letter of celebration to yourself in your eighties. What would you have to do to make all of those dreams come true?

_____

_____

_____

_____

_____

_____

_____

_____

_____

_____

_____

_____

_____

_____

_____

_____

_____

_____

_____

_____

WHY I WRITE

—●—

Write down who you were, who you are,
and what you want to remember.
Natalie Goldberg

In this section, we will discover the power of journaling from the experience of others.

Each of these short passages describes the importance of taking time to document the happenings in life.

For some, journaling is a way to capture the activities that make up the daily life.

For others, journaling is a way to explore the emotions that come through trials and challenges in life.

As you'll read in the following pages, keeping a journal can help with planning and finding purpose.

Journaling can take the form of list-making or even writing down one or two-word bullet points.

Sometimes, journaling can be thought of as a gift: a collection of stories and memories we can keep to ourselves or share with the people we love.

I want to thank these special people for taking the time to contribute their insight and wisdom to this project.

My hope is their perspective will be a blessing to you.

Finding Light in the Darkness

When I wake up and have what I call "a grey morning"—not shutters closed, lights out depths of my worst depression, but more of a morning that is giving me a warning, like the depression monster is here, it's growing; it wants to be fed. I see it as a monster or a grey fog bubbling up in front of me, trying to block my light.

And when I see it, I immediately start writing.

It starts simply. I write my husband; I write my therapist, and I write my mom. Immediately, the grey starts to dissipate.

Then I start writing in a journal. I express what I see, feel, taste, smell, and sense.

I don't try to imagine what triggered it this particular morning or force any change. Yet, I'll use this journal to keep shining a light on the fog, and I'll share my journaling with others. It acts like a low beam and starts cutting through the depression, allowing me to see.

Journaling allows me to see the path of light—it reminds me there is light.

And when the depression fog/monster lifts fully, I can go back and use my journal as a guide for my team and me to better understand the triggers, the tools that help get me out, and those mental wellness clues are found in the journal that help navigate the next darker adventure.

—**Ginger Zee,** chief meteorologist at ABC News, *New York Times* bestselling author of *Natural Disaster, A Little Closer to Home,* and the *Chasing Helicity* series.

Do you pay attention to your mental health? Do you have a strategy for taking action when you recognize signs of anxiety or depression? After years of professional therapy and enhanced self-awareness, Ginger Zee uses journaling as a tool in her battle with depression. How could you embrace this strategy in searching for light in your times of darkness? Can you find comfort and hope by reading your own feelings written in your own handwriting?

_____

_____

_____

_____

_____

_____

_____

_____

_____

_____

_____

_____

_____

_____

_____

_____

_____

_____

_____

_____

A Lifetime of Journaling

When I was about twelve, I fell in love with a cute boy named Steve which created a lot of new emotions inside of me. A few weeks later, he broke my heart by sitting with a different girl in the school cafeteria, leaving me with lots of other emotions - ones I wasn't sure how to process. I knew I felt rotten, but I didn't want to talk about it or share with anyone - and thus began my life-long appreciation for journaling. I realized, gratefully, that writing down my thoughts helped me move past the more negative aspects of a situation, to unload my sadness onto the page and hopefully leave it there instead of carrying it around. For me, journaling is like talking to a trusted friend, one who never judges or offers un-solicited advice. One who is always there to listen whole-heartedly.

My father passed away when I was just fourteen, and my mother when I was twenty-six, so journaling during those times was a lifeline. None of my friends had lost parents yet and few people could really understand what I was going through, even though they tried to be supportive. So I wrote about the memories I had of my family, of cherished childhood moments, vacations and hol-idays. And I wrote about some of the more difficult times and the complicated relationships that many of us have with our parents. Ultimately this became like a time-capsule on the page.

As time went by, I also wrote down all my hopes, and plans, and goals for my own future, kind of like a bucket-list/master-to-do list for my life. Everything seemed more possible if I wrote it down.

After I got married and had two daughters, I journaled about all the wonderful happy times we shared, and also about all of the crazy, frustrating times that come with being a wife and mother. There was definitely more good than bad and I'm glad I took the time to write things down that I would have otherwise forgotten. Those days when your kids are little go by so fast it's nice to be able to go back and remember.

And now, as a divorced, empty-nester, I find that keeping a journal is as cathartic as ever. My bucket/to-do list has definitely changed but writing things down is still very much like therapy for me, and helps me organize my thoughts and emotions. It helps me set aside the worries that are unhelpful and destructive, and instead allows me to focus on all the blessings I have all around me. As I re-read old pages, I can see how far I've come and how much I learned. And in a few cases, it's shown me some unhealthy patterns that I need to keep working on. Through journaling, I remind myself that every day is a new chance to become a better version of myself.

—**Tracy Brogan,** *Wall Street Journal* and *USA Today* bestselling author
and Amazon Publishing Diamond Award Winner for *Bell Harbor*
and *Trillium Bay* series

Has journaling been a part of your life for decades? If you are like Tracy and have been writing down the "highs and lows" through many seasons in life, dig out those old journals and spend time re-reading the entries. See if you can identify survival tactics that worked for you in past difficulties, and write down a plan for incorporating those same strategies into a plan for today.

_____

_____

_____

_____

_____

_____

_____

_____

_____

_____

_____

_____

_____

_____

_____

_____

_____

_____

_____

_____

Creating a Living Journal

The importance of writing down the now for the future is vitally important for both the writer and the soul. This gives us a living journal—an artistic and spiritual guide—of where we've been and where we're going. And we cannot know where we're going without understanding where we've been.

—Wade Rouse, international bestselling author of
The Clover Girls (Pen Name: Viola Shipman)

What is happening in your life *now*?

As an author, Wade embraces the importance of writing things down. What would your living journal document as the special part of today? How can remembering where you've been give you promise or hope for where you are going?

_____

_____

_____

_____

_____

_____

_____

_____

_____

_____

_____

_____

_____

_____

_____

_____

_____

_____

_____

_____

Find Your Voice and Choose Wisely

In the middle of my deepest and darkest struggle, I found my voice. It wasn't a raging scream or a pleading request, uttered in my time of trouble. It was a rush of thoughts and feelings only understood once I took them pen to paper, written word by written word.

I had always wanted to be a writer, but I didn't have any content. I'd start writing and crumble it up or delete the digital file. But then my life fractured into a million pieces, and the only outlet I had was writing. The content flowed, originating from my chaotic thoughts and swirling feelings. And journaling became a healing process.

When we're hurting, some of our actions are responsible and healthy responses. But others tend to be emotional reactions, times when we just lose control. Through journaling, I learned to connect my thoughts and feelings with my actions, allowing me time to slow down and respond well every time.

My journal entries morphed into a working template to help me manage, and I've used this template ever since:

- I feel . . . (list out your emotions)
- When I feel this way, I think . . . (list out your thoughts)
- When I think this, I tend to . . . (describe your specific actions).

I feel betrayed.

When I feel betrayed, I think this relationship isn't worth it.

When I think this way, I tend to scream, yell, and storm out, leaving a productive conversation too early.

Day after day, I used this template to cope, understand my actions, choice wisely the next time, and eventually heal.

I pray this template serves you well should you decide to try it during your most difficult transitions and seasons of life.

—**Cortney Donelson,** owner and principal writer, vocem, LLC, founder of GirlStory magazine, and author of *Clay Jar, Cracked: When We're Broken But Not Shattered*

How do you express your emotions in times of challenge? Do you allow turbulent thoughts to circulate in your brain, or do you "let them out?" Cortney's step-by-step template offers you a productive way to explore deep emotions and conflict. What is causing you the greatest amount of pain right now? Use this template to unravel your difficulties and look for a hopeful solution.

_____

_____

_____

_____

_____

_____

_____

_____

_____

_____

_____

_____

_____

_____

_____

_____

_____

_____

_____

_____

A Journal of Prayers

My husband died by suicide on December 13, 2001. His family (fifty-five members) walked away from me after the last shovel of dirt was pitched on his grave. I felt that his family knew why my husband died by suicide but chose not to share that information with me.

When I first started writing in a journal, my purpose was to document the life that I lived with my husband in search of the things that I should have questioned to understand better the man I married. I discovered that he lived a double life, had multiple affairs, and was allegedly part of the Philadelphia Mafia.

Anger was destroying me from the inside out. I soon discovered that the only being I could turn to for help was the one that I hated the most . . . God.

I am not sure why I decided to have a love-hate relationship with God. My best guess was that I felt He could have shown me signs of my husband's depression and did not.

I started each page with "Dear God, Hear my prayers . . ." I wrote to God about my questions, concerns, fears, lack of self-worth, and so much more. Many times, I graced pages with so many tears that I could barely read the smeared ink.

As I continued to write in my journals, directly to God, I found peace and discovered more of myself. I found the courage, determination, self-love, and faith to honor who I was despite any circumstances. I confirmed that God loves me and always has my back, even when I do not feel His presence.

One day, I asked God to write back to me. I did not know if my request was crazy or profound. To my amazement, God wrote back to me through my head, heart, and soul. Journaling brought me closer to God and helped me become the person I am today.

—**Janet V. Grillo,** author of *God Promised Me Wings to Fly: Life for Survivors After Suicide*

Are you suffering from emotional pain in your life? Is there a re-lationship that is broken that you desperately want to heal? Janet created a special prayer to use as a daily prompt to ask God to show her grace and comfort. How can you find hope and peace in the same way?

_____

_____

_____

_____

_____

_____

_____

_____

_____

_____

_____

_____

_____

_____

_____

_____

_____

_____

_____

_____

_____

Track of Life's Special Details

As the author of numerous journals, I know the importance of keeping track of the details that may otherwise be forgotten in our crazy-busy lives.

Track records are important, don't you think?

I've always felt that revisiting the grace notes (my term for everyday miracles) that Papa God has already done in our lives is crucial to helping us develop miracle memory (like muscle memory) so we'll default to trust rather than fear when crises arise.

Journals are a great way to keep Papa God's track record right in front of us.

—**Debora M. Coty,** award-winning author of over thirty inspirational books, including the bestselling *Too Blessed to be Stressed* series.
www.DeboraCoty.com

Second by second.

Minute by minute.

Hour by hour.

Day by day.

Life goes by so fast. Those seconds, minutes and hours can become a blur.

As Debora encourages, can you recognize the details you don't want to forget? How can you commit to writing them down?

_____

_____

_____

_____

_____

_____

_____

_____

_____

_____

_____

_____

_____

_____

_____

Writing Down and RELEASING The Pain

The first time I remember journaling as an adult was after my brother died, I was nineteen. The purple hardcover notebook had a quote that I can't recall now, but I'm certain it was meant to ignite hope, scrawled across the front. I opened to the first page and wrote the words that I would use to begin every entry after: Dear Johnny.

Over the next few years, I journaled through my grief, highs and frequent lows, confusion, sadness, and general life updates in those entries to my brother. I wrote about our childhood memories and when things reminded me of him. I journaled about the things I was doing to try to somehow right the wrongs of his early death, like giving presentations to local schools and studying substance abuse therapy in college.

I thought documenting it all would help keep his memory alive—proof that someone was once so loved and so terribly missed. Maybe I'd share it with others who could learn from it and more importantly, learn about him.

But nearly a decade later, when I was preparing to move to a new house with my husband, I came across my Dear Johnny journal. I lifted it out of a box crammed with photos and cards and mementos, which I had saved to cherish his twenty-four years of life. That little purple journal now felt like a hundred pounds in my hands, holding the weight of all the pain and sadness from that dark season of my life. I briefly opened the cover and thumbed through the pages, taking in glimpses of words and phrases that I only partially remembered writing. *It felt more like reading a stranger's journal than my own.*

I realized then that the journal was never meant to be saved forever. It wasn't meant for others' eyes. It wasn't even meant for my own. Filling those pages through my grief had helped me process all the emotions, sadness, and guilt that flooded that painful season of my life. It had served its purpose. It helped me to let go, release the pain, until I slowly emerged to a place of peace. I remember feeling a sense of relief and gratitude as I tossed that journal into the trash.

For me—and I hope you find this too—journaling is no longer just a way to work through difficult seasons or document special memories. It's a daily practice I do that brings clarity, focus, and intention to my hectic days as a business owner and mom of three.

In the morning, I start my day by journaling my priorities and intentions for the day. In the evening, I review what went well and what could be improved. In the Stoic philosophy, journaling is an exercise in self-examination and used to build consistent habits, strong character, and a clear mind.

Journaling isn't just a way to document the memories of our days; it's a way to gain clarity and create intention so we can live our days to the fullest.

—**Emily Richett,** founder, lead publicist, Happy PR

What is your greatest period of grief? Was it the loss of a loved one? The loss of a relationship? Can you imagine writing out your deepest, darkest pain in full detail and just like Emily, one day finding it therapeutic and healing to throw those words away?

_____

_____

_____

_____

_____

_____

_____

_____

_____

_____

_____

_____

_____

_____

_____

_____

_____

_____

_____

_____

_____

_____

_____

Precious Moments and Memories

Remember how long summer used to feel when you were a kid?

Endless days stretching out in front of you. Now, with my older daughter, Delaney, home from college for the summer, and my younger daughter, Teegan, getting ready to start her senior year of high school, it doesn't feel like that anymore.

It feels like time keeps speeding up, and I keep trying to hold onto each moment!

Writing helps me remember the funny things my younger one says and the different baking recipes my older girl has tried out.

I wrote a lot when Delaney first left for college—wrote about how much I missed her, how it was a bigger adjustment than I thought.

I know it will be just as hard when Teegan goes next year, but I can read those pages from before and know I'll get through it—know they'll come back for holidays and summer break—no matter how quickly it goes by.

—**Michele DeSelms,** news anchor and journalist, WOOD-TV

The process of "emptying the nest" happens in waves, especially as a child leaves home for college. Breaks in the college calendar will allow the nest to temporarily fill up before emptying out again. Take time to write about these times of transition. Like Michele, would reading about your own experiences during these times of transition comfort you and get you ready for the "next time?"

_____

_____

_____

_____

_____

_____

_____

_____

_____

_____

_____

_____

_____

_____

_____

_____

_____

_____

_____

_____

A Gratitude Journal

After I dropped my son off at college, I was a heaping mess. I returned home and immediately journaled every ounce of pain and loneliness I was feeling, and he hadn't even been gone a whole day. I even wrote about my regret in forcing him to eat asparagus as a kid when he hated it. My journals have always been like a confidante where I can release my joys and sorrows, desires, and disappointments.

I have a separate gratitude journal I write in daily to highlight the abundance of blessings God gives me every day. This helps me focus on the positive things in life and not wallow in the negative. How much more lovely life is when we see how blessed we are.

I've kept journals for decades to unload everything on my mind so I can relieve stress, lament grief, and express gratefulness. Journaling is so healing. And I enjoy reading past entries from years ago. These entries are like being reunited with my younger self, and I can see how life has evolved. My journals capture real thoughts in real time. These journals have become trusted friends, with memories that don't fade.

—Jennifer Feuerstein, associate state director, AARP Michigan

Writing in a journal is a great way to express the painful times in our lives. But, have you considered keeping a gratitude journal? How could you benefit by embracing Jennifer's strategy of intentionally writing down the blessings in your life? What are you grateful for today?

_____

_____

_____

_____

_____

_____

_____

_____

_____

_____

_____

_____

_____

_____

_____

_____

_____

_____

_____

_____

_____

The Power of Writing It Down

Journaling has been a lifelong habit. I am very visual and need to see thoughts or ideas written on paper to process them. When I am trying to figure out the reason behind being worried or sad or angry, I write. By the time I finish, I have come up with what event or fear caused my emotions—and likely a solution as well.

Journaling is a habit I love and will forever be a part of my routine and success.

I also use journaling for planning. Every Sunday night, I make a worry list and use it to make my calendar for the week. I group my worries into categories: personal, work, and other goals, such as big projects with ongoing research studies or papers to write. The personal list includes such basic concerns as bills, kids' events, and plans, vet appointments, household chores, or plans for an upcoming trip. This category also includes daily exercise, appointments, the daily menu, and shopping lists. My work list will include meetings and necessary tasks to prepare, goals for the workweek, and scheduled patient care hours. This weekly habit allows me to process events from the week before and gets me organized and prepared for the upcoming week. More importantly, the list gets worries out of my brain before I try to sleep. I sleep knowing that everything is handled, or that it's not important enough to include in the list.

I love to journal about my constant flow of goals and ideas using bubble-writing. I start with a big sheet of clean paper and a fresh pencil and write either the end goal or a starting thought. I do this for speeches, events, goals, or spaces I want to create, such as my garden. When I created my new medical office, I first wrote and circled words, including "calm, peaceful, and inviting," and from these came the overview of the flow and look and feel for my office. I believe that for a desired event to happen, such as a great patient experience, all must be well thought out in advance. The design team used my bubble writings to create the dream board to create a true "Women's Health experience." Bubble-writing is my way to work out what I want in order to make goals come to life.

I write to myself to live the life I want.

—Dr. Diana Bitner, MD, NCMP, FACOG, chief medical officer,
True Women's Health

Have you considered the potential of keeping a journal to help you make plans for the future? Dr. Bitner shares the power of easing worries and unleashing creative energy by regularly writing in a journal for a daily, weekly, or monthly planner. Can you tame your stress the same way?

_____

_____

_____

_____

_____

_____

_____

_____

_____

_____

_____

_____

_____

_____

_____

_____

_____

_____

_____

_____

_____

An Appointment For Journaling

As a writing coach, I discovered that what my students (of all ages) struggle with the most is finding/making time to write.

We come to writing thinking we need to set aside long periods of time to write.

Just the opposite is true.

I encourage writers to start with just ten minutes. Most people can find ten minutes.

What to write? That's where journaling comes in.

Journal about anything or something for ten minutes, then stop or continue if you're on a roll.

It won't take long, and you'll be looking forward to your journaling time.

—**Tricia L. McDonald,** owner/operator, Splattered Ink Press, author of *Life With Sally* series, *Quit Whining Start Writing*, and *The Sally Squad: Pals to the Rescue*

When something is important to us, we make time for it. As Tricia explains, creating a specific time to *start* writing on a regular basis is a big part of meeting the challenge. By scheduling an appointment, you may find it easier to fall into the routine of documenting those memories in life. Your window of time may start small, with just five or ten minutes. As with most things in life, the key is to just take the first step. (Or in this case, write the first word!) I encourage you to write for ten minutes about any topic in the space below.

_____

_____

_____

_____

_____

_____

_____

_____

_____

_____

_____

_____

_____

_____

_____

_____

_____

_____

_____

Creating a New Habit

I'm new to journaling, and I've managed to keep a five-year daily journal going for over a year now. I am, of course, not perfect at it. I frequently miss days and find the need to go back and reconstruct things. Even when that happens, I don't let it stop my flow of thought. I just go ahead and write down what I think happened that day, as I know memory isn't perfect and sometimes it's best to put down what's on your mind at the moment anyway because chances are, those are the things you're thinking or even worrying about from day to day.

As I go back and see what I've entered, it gives me a sense of perspective. Maybe it's just for a few moments each day that I gain this perspective, but even for that time, it's a good mental and spiritual practice. Sometimes, the sense of perspective comes back to me during the day in fleeting moments. It helps me see the continuity of life, its consistency, and how things keeping going regardless of where my head might be at any one moment. I'm so appreciative of this practice and can't imagine stopping now.

—**David Morris,** former publisher, Zondervan Publishing

Are you someone who has never kept a journal or diary? What are the steps you could take to make writing in a journal a regular part of your life? How long do you think it would take for you to become like David, someone who has only kept a journal for a year but now misses the activity if he occasionally skips a day? Make a commitment to either write a journal entry at the beginning of the day or before you head to bed at night. Ask yourself, "What do I want to accomplish today?" or "What did I do today that I want to remember?"

_____

_____

_____

_____

_____

_____

_____

_____

_____

_____

_____

_____

_____

_____

_____

_____

_____

The Book in Each Of Us

Anyone who tells you their life has gone exactly as planned is someone not to be trusted with your house keys. We are, each of us, a collision of circumstances, careening through life with neither headlights to illuminate the way nor brakes to keep from bumping into things. That is what makes us and our time on earth so fascinating.

When I was on the road, peddling my book and speaking to groups on the joy of writing, I billed my talk "The book in each of us" because each of us is living a life worth remembering. Your kids would far rather know the details of your life than to inherit the leftovers, such as the china, the silverware, or the lawn mower. Okay, maybe the mower. And your stories.

Write your stories down, either as a daily journal or in little episodic memories of the high and low points of your life. Skill isn't necessary, and worrying about spelling, grammar, punctuation, penmanship, shame, or guilt is not a valid reason to take your life story to the grave.

And since the first sentence is always the hardest, skip the first sentence.

—**Buck Matthews,** former WOOD-TV weatherman and television personality, author of *Getting Here* and *Uncommon Women*

Could you imagine writing in a journal to become a series of thoughts and ideas to be shared with your children (or even grandchildren)? Does Buck's perspective of "the book in each of us" inspire you to create your own literary time capsule? What comes to mind when you think of others reading the story of "your life," written in your own words?

_____

_____

_____

_____

_____

_____

_____

_____

_____

_____

_____

_____

_____

_____

_____

_____

_____

_____

_____

List Making is Journaling

I'm a list-maker, not a keeper of journals. I tried to keep a diary as an adolescent, but it was mostly rants against my younger brothers, who found it and wrote mean stuff back. Recently I found a lovely, thick, red journal with two entries: one from 2004 and one from 2007.

I've always felt a little guilty about not journaling, like maybe it was a thing "real" writers did, so I must not be a "real" writer.

Wrong.

I'm a real writer who makes lists. I've embraced list-making, using books made for long-form journaling that offer plenty of room for bullet points, numbering, or little stars to mark each point.

I also use my Franklin Planner to list out what I need to do each day.

Writing long-hand lets me think a bit more about what I want to say, but listing helps me not get tangled up in grammatically correct sentences and thus miss the point of recording my thoughts.

Also, eight quick bullet points takes way less time than laboriously recording five pages of thoughts.

I've got stuff to do!

A couple of examples of recent lists: Why I Want to Lose Weight; Why I Don't Want to Lose Weight; I'm Mad About _____ for These Reasons; If I Could Say What I'm Thinking to _____, This is What I Would Say; Long-Term Goals.

Listing lets me release anger and frustration, think through the true reasons behind my feelings, prioritize short- and long-term goals, and find positives amid negative circumstances—all benefits of journaling as well. Not to mention use the twenty or so empty journals and notebooks taking up space in my office.

My next list: All the Reasons I Like List-Making!

—**Ann Byle,** freelance writer, owner, AB Writing Services, and author of
Christian Publishing 101

What comes to mind when you think about keeping a journal? If the thought of long-form writing line after line of perfect (or imperfect) prose comes to mind and the task seems too daunting, could you take a page from the playbook of Ann Byle? Get started by making lists or even writing down bullet points. Just a few simple words from each day can preserve a memory! Start here:

_____

_____

_____

_____

_____

_____

_____

_____

_____

_____

_____

_____

_____

_____

_____

_____

_____

_____

_____

_____

_____

_____

Journaling to Slow Down and Find Clarity

I journal to figure out what I'm really thinking and feeling. My life is busy. I bet yours is too. Life is full of the good and bad, the exciting and boring, the easy and complex. At the end of many days, I feel overwhelmed by all that's happened in just twenty-four hours. I often feel tired from juggling work, family, and other responsibilities simultaneously. It seems that I rarely have time to process the various emotions—sometimes strong emotions—that come from a full life.

Journaling is an activity that forces me to slow down. Journaling by hand—putting pen to paper—requires more time than it takes to fire off an email. It also requires more thought than quickly picking a funny meme for social media or texting an emoji.

Journaling gently demands that you stop doing everything else, sit quietly, and think. This simple practice starts to sort my thoughts and feelings.

Sometimes, I will journal a lot. I'll record a whole experience, just as it happened, so that I can step back from it and observe the event for all its good and bad. It takes pages and pages.

Sometimes, I will journal just a little. A few quick sentences that capture my feelings about an event or a person.

Sometimes, I record questions I'm not ready to ask or prayers I'm not ready to say out loud.

Sometimes, I journal every day, and sometimes, I go for weeks without journaling.

The length and frequency of my entries aren't important. What's important is that I've slowed down and given myself time to process my thoughts and feelings.

In this way, journaling leads me toward a healthier, happier life.

—**A.L. Rogers,** writer and editor, Elwood House, LLC

Do you make time to reflect on your life? Do you ever slow down and just spend time in thought and meditation? In his time of journaling, Andy Rogers describes the process of sitting quietly and thinking about what's going on in his life. How can you embrace this strategy of taking out a pen and notepad to document life in your own handwriting? I encourage you to start here. Sit. Think. Then write.

_____

_____

_____

_____

_____

_____

_____

_____

_____

_____

_____

_____

_____

_____

_____

_____

_____

_____

_____

Conclusion

A journey of 1,000 miles begins with a single step.
Lao Tzu

This famous quote was probably written between the fourth and sixth centuries by a famous Chinese philosopher, but the phrase can be applied to every human in any stage in life.

It suggests the toughest part of accomplishing anything is the point at the beginning. Maybe you have discovered this to be true. Once something is started, the rest of the task will follow more easily.

For the transition into the Empty Nest stage, the beginning of that one-thousand-mile journey takes place on the day your young adult child moves out of the nest, leaving home to begin his or her own journey in life. Even though we are left behind, that moment is really "step one" in our new journey.

I hope this journal and its companion book have helped you understand that the next stage in your life has the potential to be the best stage.

I hope that you realize you have plenty of company in your Empty Nest, but that when you feel all alone, you can draw on your own strength and the memories of the past to plan for a promising future.

Brighter Skies **ARE** Ahead.

About the Author

As a television meteorologist, **Terri DeBoer** has delivered West Michigan's "wake up" weather for three decades. She also co-hosts a daily lifestyle show, *eightWest*.

Terri's public journey through the seasons in life, from on-air pregnancies to the marriages of two children and becoming a grandmother, gives her a special connection with other moms and grandmothers. She now shares lessons from her most challenging season of life: adjusting to the quieter life in an Empty Nest.

Terri resides in Byron Center, Michigan. Connect with Terri at www.terrideboer.com.

A free ebook edition is available with the purchase of this book.

To claim your free ebook edition:

1. Visit MorganJamesBOGO.com
2. Sign your name CLEARLY in the space
3. Complete the form and submit a photo of the entire copyright page
4. You or your friend can download the ebook to your preferred device

Morgan James BOGO™

A **FREE** ebook edition is available for you or a friend with the purchase of this print book.

CLEARLY SIGN YOUR NAME ABOVE

Instructions to claim your free ebook edition:
1. Visit MorganJamesBOGO.com
2. Sign your name CLEARLY in the space above
3. Complete the form and submit a photo of this entire page
4. You or your friend can download the ebook to your preferred device

Print & Digital Together Forever.

Snap a photo

Free ebook

Read anywhere

CPSIA information can be obtained
at www.ICGtesting.com
Printed in the USA
BVHW030921100921
616194BV00010B/16